The Story of the DINOSAURS

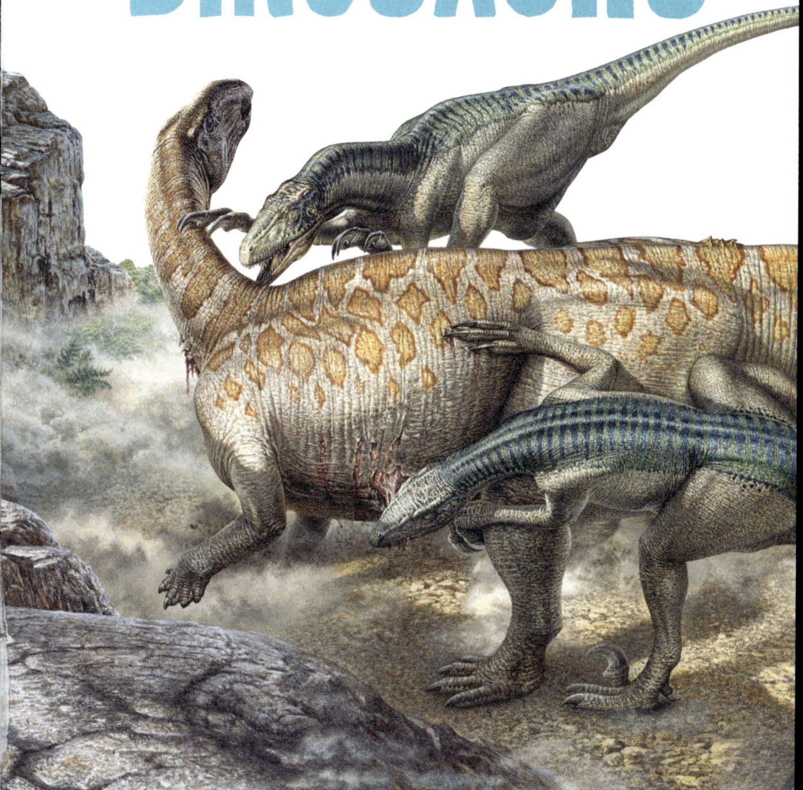

Contents

Long, long ago

Long, long ago there were no tigers or elephants, no seals or whales, and no people. But, there were - dinosaurs! From about 230 million years ago, they ruled the Earth in the time we call the Age of the Dinosaur.

Flesh-chomping *Tyrannosaurus* (tie-RAN-oh-sore-us) was one of the biggest meat-eating dinosaurs, more than 12 metres long.

Speedy *Ornithomimus* (orn-ITH-oh-MEE-mus) was able to race along at over 60 kilometres per hour, the same speed as a racehorse.

Leaf-munching *Iguanodon* (ig-WHA-noh-don) was one of the most common big dinosaurs. It was as big as an elephant.

The first living things

Planet Earth formed over 4,500 million years ago. The first living things, 3,500 million years ago, looked like tiny specks in the sea. Gradually living things became bigger and more complex.

Dimetrodon (die-MEET-roe-don) lived 270 million years ago, before the Age of the Dinosaur. Its tall sail of skin on its back, held up by bony spines, soaked up the sun's heat so it could warm up and become active quickly.

Nothosaurs (NO-thow-SORES) lived 220 million years ago, early in the Age of the Dinosaur. They were reptiles but not dinosaurs. They swam in the sea and ate fish and other water creatures.

Dimorphodon (die-MORE-foe-don) lived 195 million years ago, during the Age of the Dinosaur. It was a type of flying reptile called a pterosaur.

Woolly mammoths lived less than one million years ago, long after the Age of the Dinosaur. They were mammals and had long fur to keep out the cold.

Mesozoic era

Dinosaurs lived during the Mesozoic Era. This had three parts, called periods. In the Triassic Period, 252-201 million years ago, the first dinosaurs were

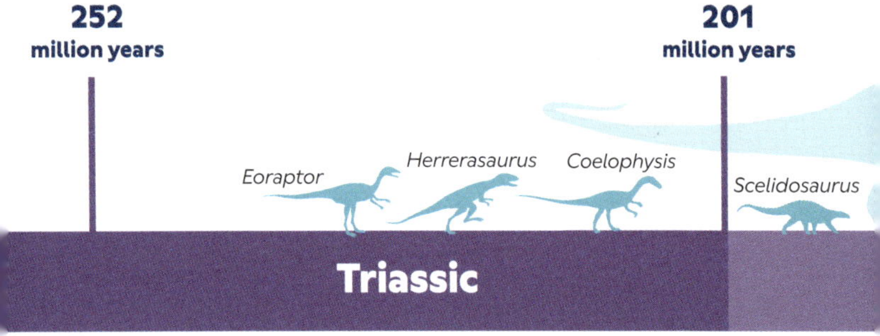

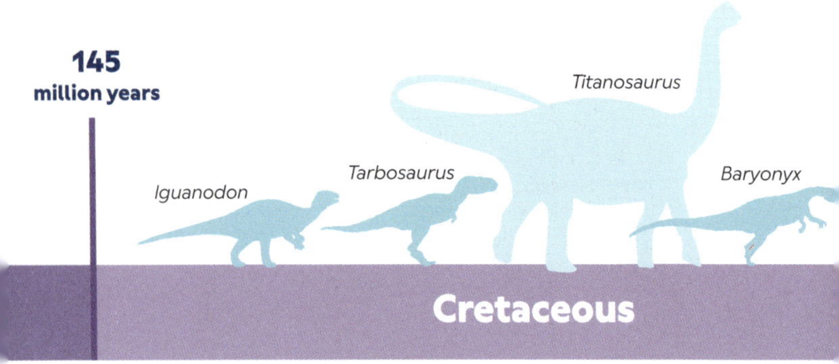

small. Both big and tiny dinosaurs lived in both the Jurassic Period, 201 to 145 million years ago, and the Cretaceous Period, 145–66 million years ago.

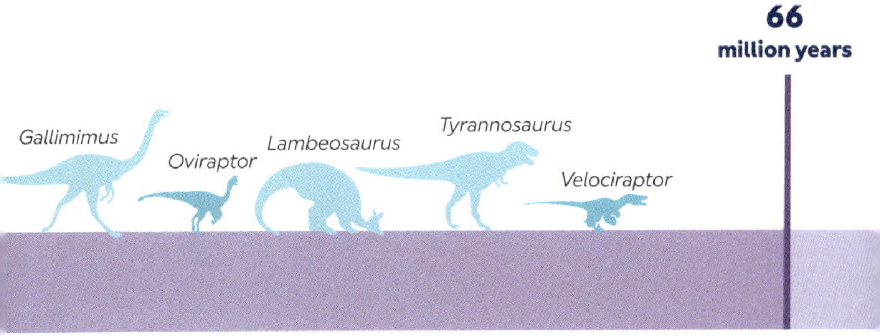

All about fossils

We can find out about dinosaurs by studying fossils of their bones, teeth, horns and claws as well as footprints and eggs that got buried and, over millions of years, turned to stone. All sorts of animals left fossils, as did plants like ferns and trees. Fossils can show us how creatures and plants lived long ago.

A fish dies. Its soft parts are eaten or rot away.

The hard parts like bones and teeth are buried by grains of sand or mud.

Over millions of years the hard parts get buried deeper and turn to stone as do the sand and mud.

The hard parts are now fossils and are revealed when weather and other forces wear away the rock around them.

Experts search rocks, such as limestone and sandstone, for fossils. These rocks formed mostly on the bottoms of rivers, lakes and seas, preserving the remains of animals and plants.

This fossil from the Jurassic Period shows that, over 150 million years ago, starfish were very similar to how they are today.

Back in the laboratory, bits of rock are cleaned from the fossil, which can take many days. This fossil of *Tyrannosaurus* is having its teeth cleaned.

Dawn of the dinosaurs

The Age of the Dinosaur began over 230 million years ago during the Triassic Period. The world was very different then. The main land masses, called continents, were joined together into one giant continent called Pangaea (pan-GEE-ah).

The edges or coasts of Pangaea were warm, with one extreme rainy season a year. Away from the sea, far inland, it was hot in summer, cold in winter, and dry for most of the year. There were huge deserts and areas of dry scrubland, and many parts of the world looked like the deserts of Arizona, USA, with spiky bushes, rocky cliffs and mountains.

Early dinosaurs

As dinosaurs spread around the world, different types evolved and they developed special features like long necks, armour and sharp teeth.

Herrerasaurus (herr-ray-rah-SORE-us) was a sharp-toothed meat-eater that ran on two powerful back legs. It grew up to 6 metres long and lived in South America about 228 million years ago.

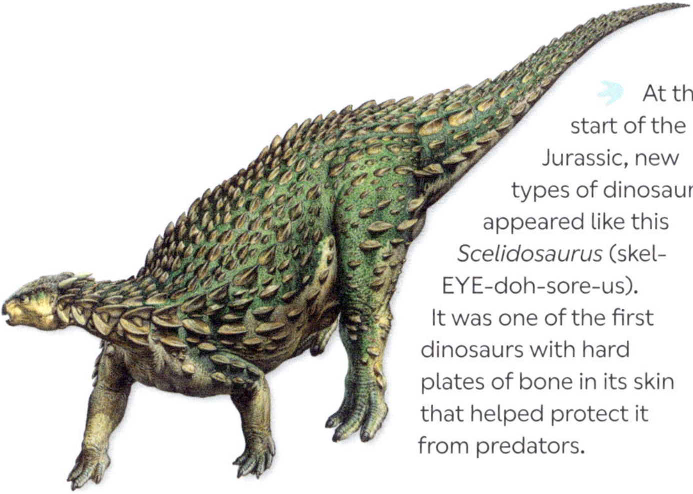

At the start of the Jurassic, new types of dinosaur appeared like this *Scelidosaurus* (skel-EYE-doh-sore-us). It was one of the first dinosaurs with hard plates of bone in its skin that helped protect it from predators.

This fossil skull is from a *Plateosaurus* (PLAT-ee-oh-SORE-us). It was one of the earliest big dinosaurs. It had many sharp-edged teeth to cut up tough plant food. It lived in Europe about 210 million years ago.

Teeming seas

As dinosaurs spread across the land during the Jurassic, they may have gone into the sea to escape enemies. No dinosaurs lived fully in the sea, but there were many other creatures like sponges, starfish and sea-lilies that did and had already been around for millions of years.

The hard, spiral shells of ammonites formed beautiful fossils. When it was alive it would have had a head with squid-like tentacles poking out of the shell.

Fossils of sea-lilies show how, during the Jurassic, these simple animals grew on floating pieces of driftwood as well as on the seabed.

The biggest belemnites were three metres long. Like ammonites, these fierce hunters had big eyes and bendy arms to grab fish and any other prey they could catch. They had a long, pointed shell in the inside of their tail.

Belemnite shells are shaped like bullets. So rocks with lots of them packed together are known as 'belemnite battlegrounds'. They suggest belemnites were very common during the Age of the Dinosaur.

Sea-going giants

During the Jurassic Period the world became warmer and more new creatures appeared. As dinosaurs conquered the lands, other reptiles conquered the seas and grew to enormous sizes.

Pliosaurs had broad, fat bodies with flippers, a short neck and a huge head. Some pliosaurs like *Liopleurodon* (lie-oh-plur-oh-don) were up to ten metres long.

Plesiosaurs were cousins of pliosaurs. They had bodies and flippers like pliosaurs but small heads and very long bendy necks. They grabbed small prey such as fish and belemnites with their many sharp teeth. *Plesiosaurus* (pleez-ee-oh-SORE-us) was up to five metres long.

Pliosaurs were the top predators in the Jurassic seas and probably fed on other marine reptiles. They had strong jaws and teeth with sharp, cutting edges. This curved fossil pliosaur tooth is as long as a pencil.

Some fish in the Jurassic seas were goldfish-sized; others grew bigger than cars. *Dapedium* (dap-ED-ee-um) was 40 centimetres long and had scales for protection and a large tail to help it swim away from predators.

Sea monsters

The continents drifted apart during the Jurassic and the Atlantic Ocean began to form as Pangaea broke up. Sea levels were higher, and warm, shallow seas covered what is now Europe. Some real sea monsters swam in the shallow seas!

Among the fastest swimmers were ichthyosaurs. They had long, slim jaws and sharp teeth and, like all other reptiles, did not have gills and so had to come to the surface to breathe. *Ichthyosaurus* (ick-THEE-oh-SORE-us) was about two metres long, with a back fin and crescent-shaped tail.

Temnodontosaurus (tem-no-DON-toe-SORE-us) was a massive ichthyosaur, over ten metres long. It ate other marine reptiles, using its huge eyes to see its prey in the dark, murky water.

Marine crocodiles also lived in these shallow seas. They swam by swishing their long, tapering tails. The crocodile *Steneosaurus* (sten-EE-oh-SORE-us) was covered in armoured plates, like modern crocodiles. It used its long, slender jaws to grab small fish and squid.

Mega-dinosaurs

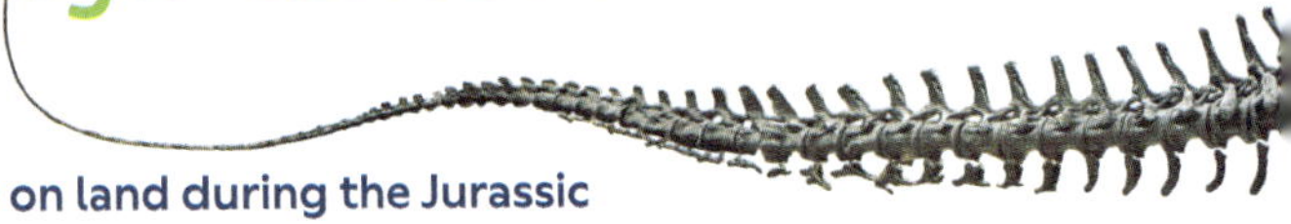

Life on land during the Jurassic was very different from today. The world was warmer, and its forests were dominated by ferns and conifer trees. Many different types of dinosaur evolved. The largest plant eaters of the Jurassic were the sauropod dinosaurs; some were the largest animals ever to live on land.

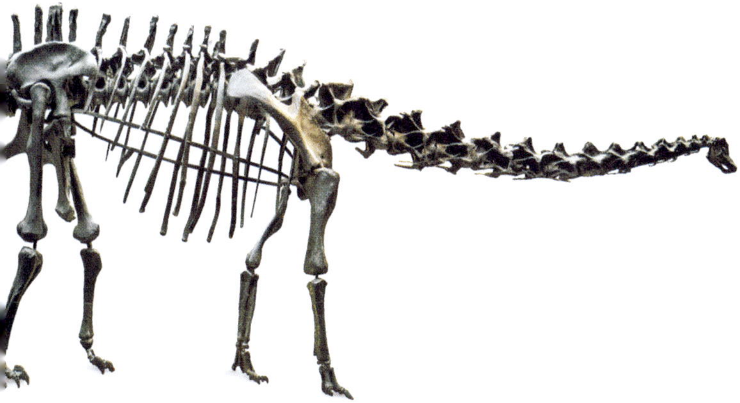

The tallest Jurassic sauropods were the American *Brachiosaurus* (brack-EE-oh-SORE-us) and its African relative *Giraffatitan* (gir-AFFA-titan). They were three times taller than a giraffe! Fossils of sauropods are often found with smoothly rounded stones bigger than your fist. Probably the dinosaurs swallowed these stones to help grind up tough plant food in their stomach.

Sauropod dinosaurs had long necks which meant they could swing their heads around and reach lots of food. These plant eaters needed to eat a huge amount of leaves to support their giant size. Having long necks allowed them to eat leaves from even the tallest trees.

Mini-dinosaurs

The small dinosaurs were slim and speedy. They could run away from enemies and hide easily. One of the smallest was *Compsognathus* (komp-sog-NATH-us), which was only a bit larger than a pet cat.

Compsognathus had long back legs for fast running, a long tail to help it turn quickly, and many sharp teeth to grab small creatures like insects and little lizards.

Only two fossils of *Compsognathus* have been found, one in Germany and one in France. In this fossil the neck is bent back so the head is over the hips and back legs.

The tiniest dinosaur fossils are babies only just hatched from the egg. The plant-eating *Maiasaura* (my-ah-SORE-ah) was just 30 centimetres long at birth, but nine metres when fully grown!

Dinosaurs take off

At the end of the Jurassic Period, new kinds of creatures took to the skies – birds. Where did they come from and were they expert fliers or clumsy gliders?

Animals and plants change gradually over time, which is known as evolution. Some small, meat-eating dinosaurs evolved by gaining special, larger feathers on their arms, turning them into simple wings. And the ones living in trees used their wings to glide from branch to branch. Over a long time their wings grew bigger and stronger, allowing them to stay in the air longer by flapping. We now call these dinosaurs birds.

Unlike birds, the tiny dinosaur *Microraptor* (MIKE-row-rap-tor) had wings on its legs as well as its arms, allowing it to glide or maybe even fly.

Fossils show that several kinds of small meat-eating dinosaurs grew feathers. However their arms were small and didn't have the wing feathers needed for flight. The dog-sized dinosaur *Dilong* (DIE-long) had fluffy feathers, which may have kept it warm in cold weather.

Archaeopteryx

***Archaeopteryx* (ark-EE-op-TER-ix) was the earliest known bird. It had teeth in its mouth, claws on its front legs and long bones in its tail. As birds developed the ability to fly, they lost these typical dinosaur features.**

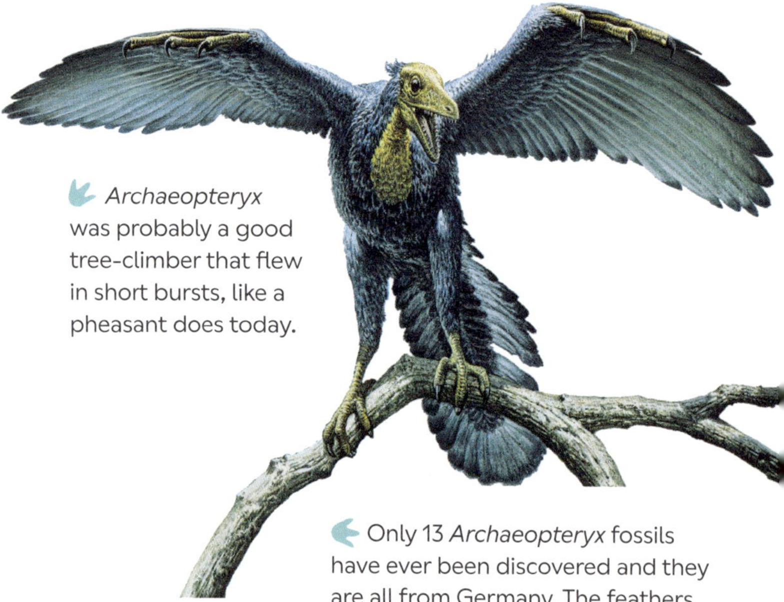

Archaeopteryx was probably a good tree-climber that flew in short bursts, like a pheasant does today.

Only 13 *Archaeopteryx* fossils have ever been discovered and they are all from Germany. The feathers and bones of this one are in the same position as they would have been when it was alive.

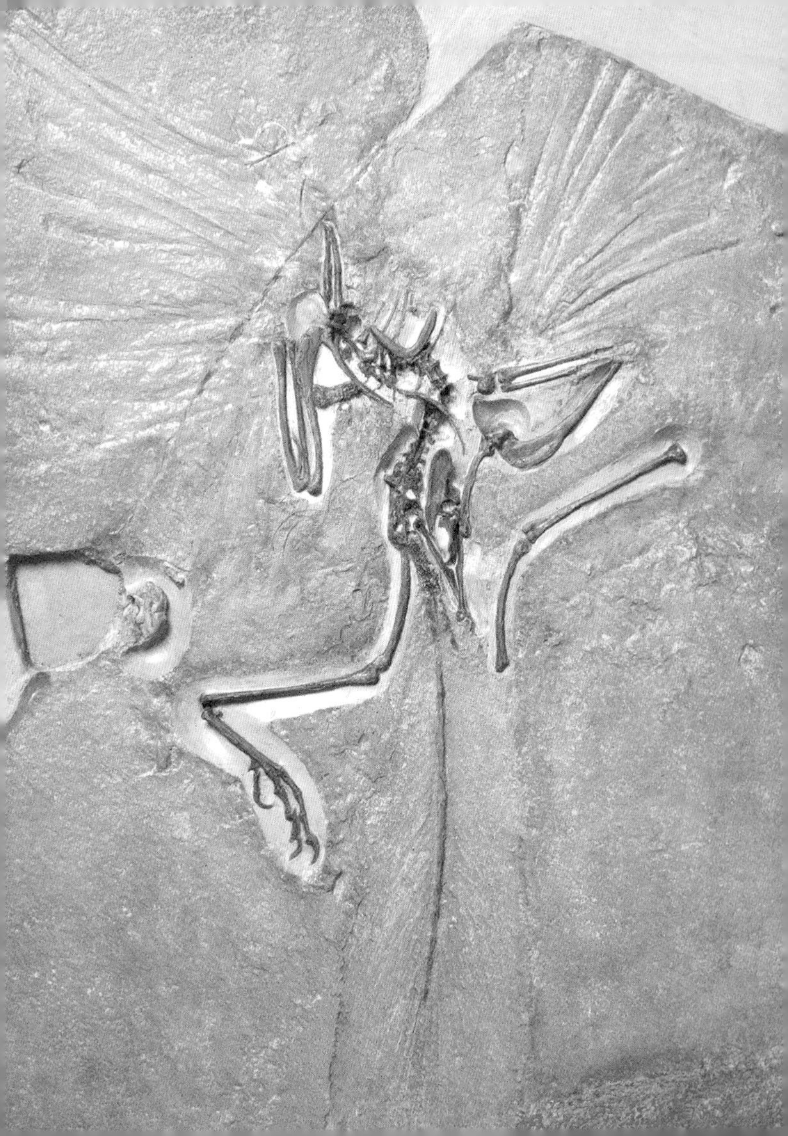

Busy skies

When the first birds swooped through Late Jurassic and Early Cretaceous skies, they were not alone. There were also flying creatures called pterosaurs which, like the dinosaurs, were reptiles.

Pterosaurs had strong arm muscles to flap their wings and fly well. They had sharp claws on their wings and on their feet too. *Anurognathus* (an-your-oh-NAY-thus) was a pterosaur that was small enough to have perched in your hand.

This fossil skull of the pterosaur *Dimorphodon* (die-MORF-oh-don) is unusually long for a pterosaur, maybe because it ate animals such as lizards and mammals.

The Jurassic pterosaur *Rhamphorhynchus* (ram-FOE-rink-us) had wings up to two metres across and a tail with a flat part (a vane) at the end. It used its sharp teeth to catch fish in the sea. Later pterosaurs had no tail, toothless beaks and developed display crests on their heads.

This fossil of the pterosaur *Pterodactylus* (ter-owe-DACK-till-us) shows its very long fourth finger bone (pointing down from the end of both arms), which supported the front of the wing.

When did they live

The Age of the Dinosaur lasted for more than 160 million years, from small meat-eaters like *Herrerasaurus* 228 million years ago, to the last big killer *Tyrannosaurus* 66 million years ago. But how do we know these dates and times?

Fossils of tiny animals called foraminifera (forams), seen here under a microscope, are used to date other fossils found with them. Forams have lived in the sea for over 500 million years.

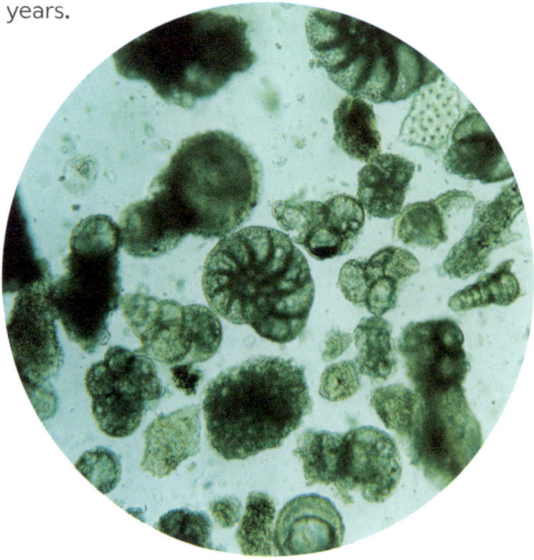

Some kinds of creatures, like ammonites, changed gradually over time and left many fossils. We can work out which ammonites lived when from the ages of the rocks that the fossils were found in. And if a dinosaur fossil is in the same age of rock as an ammonite fossil, then we know it is about the same age.

Experts use CT scanners to see inside fossils without damaging them. This CT scan of an *Archaeopteryx* fossil skull, shows a space where its brain was. The shape of the space shows how well developed the brain parts were for seeing, hearing and balancing.

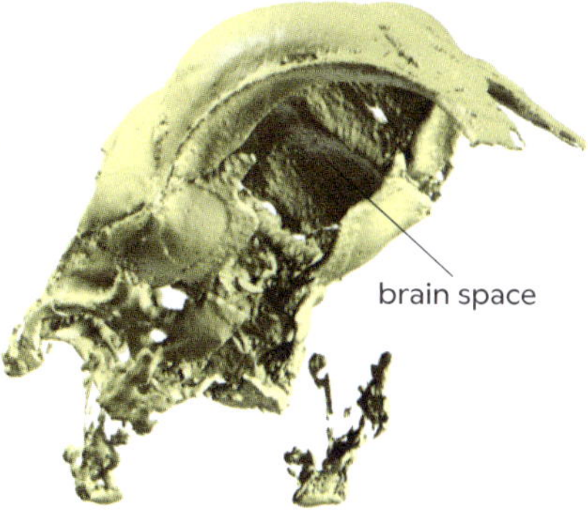

The plant-eaters

In all creatures, the size and shape of the mouth and teeth are suited to the kinds of food they eat. Long sharp teeth are good for grabbing and tearing up animal prey. Wide flat-topped teeth are best for munching plants. Dinosaurs had many different shapes of mouth and teeth, which give clues to the food they ate.

Diplodocus (DI-plod-oh-kuss) had thin, straight, peg-like teeth that were no use for chewing hard plants. The teeth were like a rake that pulled leaves off stems so it could grind them up in its stomach.

The strong teeth of the plant-eating dinosaur *Pelorosaurus* (pel-oh-ROW-sore-us) had sharp edges that could cut up hard plant food.

Duck-bill dinosaurs, like *Edmontosaurus* (ed-MON-toe-sore-us), had hundreds of teeth to help them chew up even the toughest plant material.

The meat-eaters

Most meat-eating dinosaurs belong to a group known as the theropods. They ran on two legs and hunted using their sharp toothed jaws and clawed arms. Theropods include the largest meat-eaters ever to walk on land and also the tiniest birds.

Allosaurus (AL-oh-saw-russ) had a jaw that could open really wide. This meant it could attack the other giant theropods it preyed on with slashing bites.

The biggest dinosaur teeth belonged to the great meat-eaters. *Tyrannosaurus* teeth were very strong and shaped roughly like a banana, allowing it to crunch through tough skin and bone.

Compsognathus had a mouth full of tiny pointed teeth and clawed grabbing arms that it used to catch small, fast-running lizards.

Some dinosaur dung formed fossils called coprolites. These can tell us what a dinosaur ate as they can contain bits of animal bone in them or, for a fish-eater, fish bones and scales.

Halfway through

About 145 million years ago, halfway through the Age of the Dinosaur, the Jurassic Period ended and the Cretaceous Period began. New kinds of plants grew – those with flowers. Some were similar to today's water-lilies and magnolias. They were a new kind of food and new animals, including new dinosaurs, evolved to eat them.

Muttaburrasaurus (MUT-a-BURR-a-SORE-us) was a plant-eating dinosaur in Australia during the Early Cretaceous. As the continents drifted apart, different kinds of dinosaurs evolved on them.

Sauropod dinosaurs in the Late Jurassic, such as *Brachiosaurus*, were huge. One group of sauropods, the titanosaurs, got bigger throughout the Cretaceous. The titanosaur, *Patagotitan* (Pa-ta-go-TIE-tan), was probably as big as seven male African elephants.

Everything evolving

As animals adapted to eat new plants, some plants developed defences against the plant-eaters, such as spines or a horrible taste, to avoid being eaten. Sometimes plants and animals evolved to work together.

Flowers like these magnolias are soft and delicate and fall apart, so fossils of them are very rare. The leaves however are more robust and fossils of leaf impressions can be found in rock.

As different types of flowers appeared, animals such as new types of beetles and early relatives of bees evolved to feed off them and pollinate them.

Flowers produce pollen, which is then taken to other flowers of the same kind to produce seeds. Today many insects, such as butterflies, fulfil the vital task of carrying pollen.

Together or alone

Today, some plant-eating animals like zebras and bison live in great herds. Others, such as rhinos and moose, stay mainly on their own. Fossils can help us to work out which dinosaurs were herd-dwellers and which probably lived by themselves.

Iguanodon and its close relatives were the most common plant-eaters of the Early Cretaceous, 125 million years ago. In Belgium, the skeletons of 38 *Iguanodon* were discovered stacked on top of one another. This suggests that they lived in herds, maybe helping each other to fight off enemies, and that they died together too, perhaps drowned in a sudden flood.

Armoured dinosaurs, known as ankylosaurs, were also Cretaceous plant-eaters. Ankylosaur fossils are usually found on their own, suggesting they didn't live in herds. They had big plates of bone over their bodies to protect them. This fossil is part of the thick, bony back of a *Euoplocephalus* (you-OH-plo-kef-ah-luss).

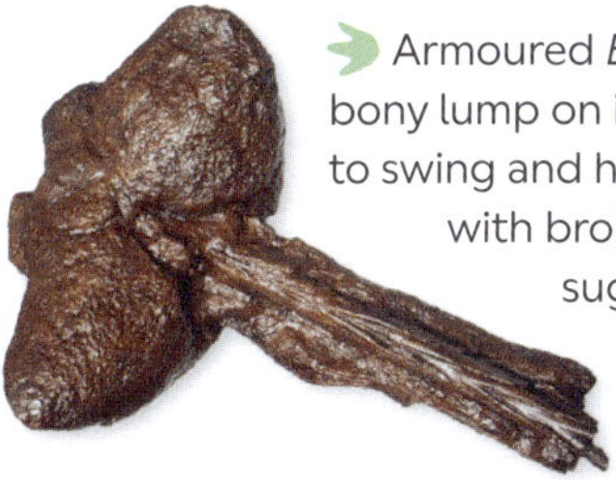

Armoured *Euoplocephalus* had a massive bony lump on its tail, which it used as a club to swing and hit its enemies. Ankylosaur fossils with broken skin and bone on their sides suggest they also hit each other.

Duck-bills galore

Towards the end of the Age of the Dinosaur, it may have been very noisy. Strange honking and trumpet-like sounds echoed through the forests and swamps.

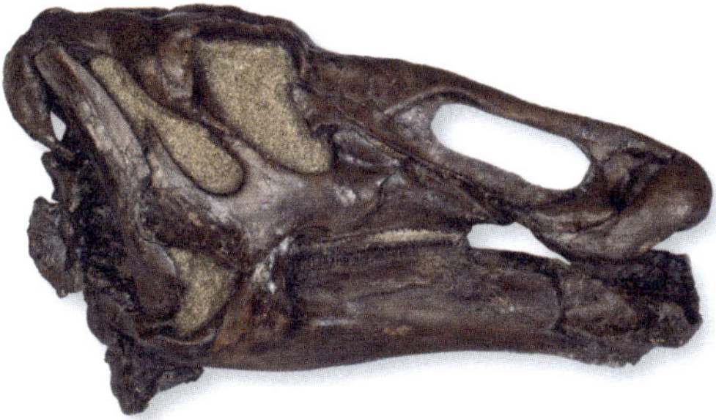

The Late Cretaceous duck-bills, known as hadrosaurs, are named after the shape of their skull. At the front the skull was wide and flat with no teeth, like a duck's bill. In life, a sharp beak for clipping plants covered this. The back of the mouth had hundreds of strong teeth for chewing tough plant food.

Many duck-bill fossils found in one place show that these dinosaurs probably lived in large groups or herds. The duck-bill *Maiasaura* (my-ah-SORE-ah) may have brought food to its babies in their nest.

Duck-bill sounds

Many duck-billed dinosaurs had odd bony shapes on their head, known as crests. Some of these crests had tubes running through them connected to the nostrils. As air blew through the crest, it may have made a loud noise. This could have been to scare enemies, attract a mate, or gather herd members together.

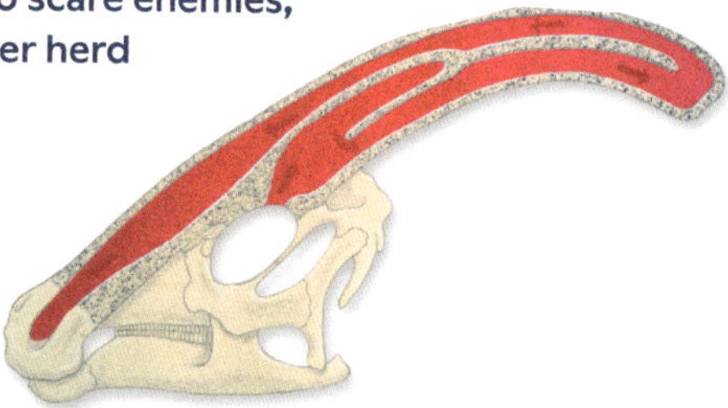

Today, elephants make a loud trumpet sound by blowing through their trunks. Did duck-bills blow through the tubes (shown above in red) in their bony skull crests to make similar sounds?

Different duck-bills had different-shaped crests. The largest crest, on *Parasaurolophus* (pa-ra-saw-ROL-off-us), was as big as you!

Duck-bill dinosaurs like *Corythosaurus* (koh-rith-OH-sore-us) had a crest like a flat wedge. Individuals of the same species could recognise each other as they had the same shaped crest.

Built for speed

Ostriches are very fast runners. In the Late Cretaceous there were dinosaurs with a similar body shape to the ostrich. These are the ornithomimids – nicknamed the ostrich-dinosaurs!

Ostrich-dinosaurs could take huge steps with their long legs. They moved the legs with strong hip muscles. Their head, neck and arms were slim and light, which helped them run faster. *Gallimimus* (gal-lee-MEEM-us) was a typical ostrich-dinosaur.

Ostriches can run almost twice as fast as a person. Maybe ostrich-dinosaurs were even faster!

This fossil of massive arms and hands - taller than a person - with very long claws is from a dinosaur called *Deinocheirus* (DINE-oh-KIRE-us). They look like the arms of an ostrich dinosaur, but it would have been huge and at least ten metres long.

Unlike its smaller relatives, the body of *Deinocheirus* was bulky and it had comparatively short legs, suggesting it was not a fast runner. Some palaeontologists think it lived in rivers and lakes like a hippo!

Horned dinosaurs

During the Cretaceous Period a new group of plant-eating dinosaurs, the ceratopsians, appeared. Towards the end of the Cretaceous these evolved sets of horns which varied between species.

In East Asia, about 75 million years ago, there were dinosaurs such as *Protoceratops* (pro-toe-KER-ah-tops) and *Velociraptor* (vel-OSS-ee-rap-tor). Today this area is the Gobi Desert. Fossils of *Protoceratops* are so common in the Gobi Desert that they are nicknamed 'The sheep of the Cretaceous'.

Protoceratops was a ceratopsian with a sharp beak and a bony frill around its neck. Its toothless beak could cut off bits of plants and, in the back of its mouth, it had strong teeth that could cut like scissors.

Psittacosaurus (SIT-ak-oh-sore-us) was quite small, at about two metres long and one metre tall. It did not have a large neck frill like the later ceratopsians.

One of the last and biggest ceratopsians was *Triceratops* (tri-KER-ah-tops). It was more than eight metres long and lived in North America. It may have used its horns in defence against predators such as *Tyrannosaurus*.

Raptors rule

Some of the most fearsome of all dinosaurs lived during Cretaceous times. They were not huge hunters like *Tyrannosaurus*. They were smaller – and probably sneakier. These are the dromaeosaurs, or raptor dinosaurs.

Not every dinosaur with 'raptor' in its name belongs to this group. Oviraptor (OH-vee-RAP-tor) had a short, toothless beak in contrast to the long, sharp, toothed jaws of the dromaeosaurs. Raptors ate meat, but we are still not sure what *Oviraptor* ate.

Originally raptors were thought to be scaly, but we now know they had feathers, like birds. This is the *Atrociraptor* (Ah-TROSS-ee-rap-tor).

Raptor dinosaurs ran on their back legs and had a deadly sharp, curved claw on each foot. The North American raptor *Deinonychus* (die-NON-i-kuss) was over three metres long. It may have hunted in a pack as shown here, attacking a *Tenontosaurus* (ten-ON-toe-sore-us).

Raptors large and small

Raptors were fast, armed with sickle claws and were smarter than most dinosaurs. This made them adaptable, and some raptors specialized in climbing, swimming and even gliding. The smaller raptors ate small prey, others ate fish, and the biggest ate other dinosaurs.

Velociraptor was surprisingly small, only two metres long. Its slender jaws were good for catching small prey but not other dinosaurs. By comparison the largest raptor, *Utahraptor* (YOO-tah-RAP-tor) grew to seven metres and had a strong, boxy skull.

Like most raptors, *Sinornithosaurus* (sine-OR-nith-oh-SORE-us) had claws on its hands and feet. It was about two metres long and lived in what is now China. It used the big curved claw on its second toe to pin down its prey.

One of the smallest raptors was the crow-sized *Microraptor* (MIKE-row-rap-tor). This tiny dinosaur was just as fierce a predator as its larger relatives. Small mammal bones and fish scales have been found fossilized in its gut.

T. rex or T. bataar

You have heard of *Tyrannosaurus rex*, but have you heard of *Tarbosaurus bataar* (TAR-bow-SORE-us bat-ARE)? The two giants were almost the same size, the same shape and lived at the same time. They were alive about 70 to 66 million years ago, when the continents had split up.

Tyrannosaurus lived in what is now North America, while *Tarbosaurus* was from East Asia. They were both massive meat-eaters, over ten metres long and weighing five tonnes, with a massive skull built for resisting extreme bite forces. Their back legs were big and powerful, yet their arms were tiny and were probably no use when it came to catching prey. *Tarbosaurus* (below) was perhaps slightly smaller.

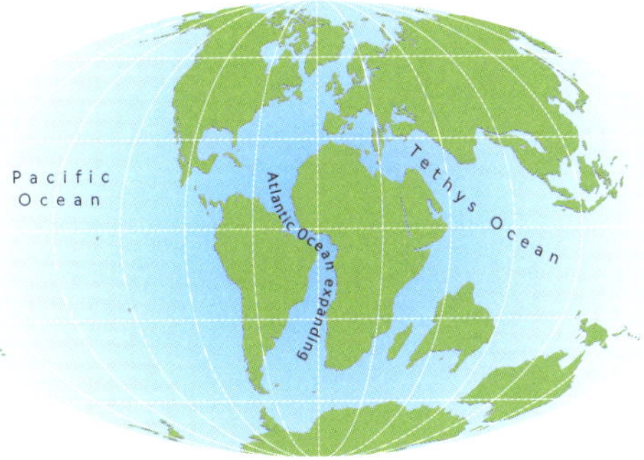

Were *Tyrannosaurus* and *Tarbosaurus* really the same kind of dinosaur? Some scientists thought they were, but they now know *Tarbosaurus* had a narrower, more rigid skull than *Tyrannosaurus*. An earlier Asian relative of the pair, *Zhuchengytyrannus* (zu-CHENG-ty-ranus), has also been discovered.

The end of the age

Just over 66 million years ago, the Cretaceous Period ended and, with it, the Age of the Dinosaur. When many kinds of living things die out at the same time, it is called a mass extinction. A giant rock from space, an asteroid, smashed into the Earth. The ash cloud dimmed the sun, killing plants around the world.

One day, 66 million years ago, the asteroid from space hit the Gulf of Mexico, triggering tsunamis in the world's oceans and starting continent-wide wildfires.

Dinosaurs like *Triceratops* had no food and so they perished. Meat-eaters that preyed on them, like *Tyrannosaurus*, also starved. Apart from dinosaurs, flying pterosaurs also died out. So did sea creatures such as plesiosaurs, mosasaurs and ammonites.

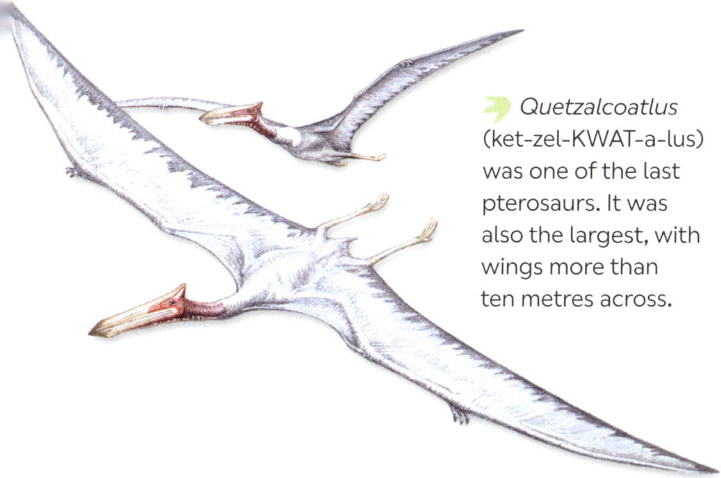

Quetzalcoatlus (ket-zel-KWAT-a-lus) was one of the last pterosaurs. It was also the largest, with wings more than ten metres across.

What didn't die out

The mass extinction killed off millions of animals and plants. But on land, smaller animals like birds, mammals, lizards, snakes and insects survived. And crocodiles and turtles also made it through, sheltering in the rivers and lakes.

Following the Age of the Dinosaur new kinds of plants and animals spread across the land. Different flowers and trees appeared and they had new kinds of mammals and birds living among them.

Many plants survived too, such as mosses, ferns, conifer trees and various flowers. Ferns are one of the first plants to recover from mass extinctions, and fern fossils are very common in the rocks after the end of the Cretaceous.

Coelacanth fishes were thought to have been extinct for 80 million years. Then a living one was caught less than 100 years ago and more have since been discovered.

Living fossils

Some living things today are very similar to their relatives from the Age of the Dinosaur. They are known as 'living fossils'. The way they behave, feed and breed helps us to work out what life was like during dinosaur times.

Today's great white shark is a puny weakling compared to its extinct cousin *Carcharodon megalodon* (car-cha-ROW-don mega-low-don), which was three times longer!

The tuatara of New Zealand looks like a lizard. But it is actually a rhynchocephalian, a group that flourished alongside the dinosaurs.

Nautiluses survived the extinction while the similar ammonites went extinct.

Fossil teeth from *Carcharodon megalodon* show that it died out around one and a half million years ago. Its teeth were similar in shape to those of great white sharks but many times bigger.

Sneaky peak to the future

After the Age of the Dinosaur, the world continued to evolve. New kinds of mammals, birds, reptiles, fish, insects, worms and other animals were joined by new types of flowers and trees. Our world is now changing faster than ever. We face problems such as global warming and pollution. People are taking over more wild places, and some animals and plants face the threat of extinction.

Our own kind, or species, is called *Homo sapiens* (hoe-mow SAP-ee-ens). Our evolution has been very fast, from living in caves and using stone tools to changing the face of the planet with cities, roads and industries in less than 20,000 years.

Rats are great pests – because they are a success of modern evolution. Their success relies on us. Rats live near humans and eat all kinds of food that we grow, store or throw away.

Animals that die today may leave fossils for the future. Who will dig them up to study them? Fossils show that a mammal type animal like us usually only lasts for two to five million years before going extinct.

Picture credits

p.2, p.49 top ©Robert Nicholls; p.3 top, right and bottom, p.24, p.26, p.36, p.40, p.42-43, p.51, p.56-57, p.62 ©John Sibbick/Science Photo Library, p.3 top, left, p.16 bottom, p.20 © Roger Harris/Science Photo Library; p.4 top © Michael Long/ Science Photo Library, p.4 bottom ©Jaime Chirinos/Science Photo Library; p.5 top ©Tim White; p.9 top ©Paul Barrett; p.9 bottom ©Lorraine Cornish; p.10-11 ©Lawrence Freytag/iStock; p.12, p.22, p.28 top, p.45 bottom © De Agostini/UIG/ Science Photo Library; p.15 top, p.18 bottom ©Graham Cripps; p.16-17 © JA Chirinos/Science Photo Library; p.25 top Christian Darkin/Science Photo Library; p.35 top ©Walter Myers/Science Photo Library; p.38 left ©Pavlo Maydikov/iStock; p.39 bottom ©James Mojonnier/iStock; p.44 bottom ©Rick Sargent/iStock; p.46 bottom John Carnemolla/iStock; p.47 bottom ©Mark P. Witton/Science Photo Library; p.48 top © Louie Psihoyos/Science Faction/Corbis; p.53 top left ©Geological Museum of China; p.54 ©Friedrich Saurer/Science Photo Library; p.56 bottom ©Mark Garlick/Science Photo Library; p.57 top ©Mauricio Anton/ Science Photo Library; p.59 bottom ©Peter Scoones/Science Photo Library; p.60 top ©Stephen Sweet/iStock; p.61 top ©Norma Cornes/iStock; p.63 top ©Oleg Kozlov/iStock; p.63 bottom ©Claudio Arnese/iStock

Unless otherwise stated images copyright of Natural History Museum, London. Every effort has been made to contact and accurately credit all copyright holders. If we have been unsuccessful, we apologise and welcome correction for future editions and reprints.

First published by the Natural History Museum, Cromwell Road, London SW7 5BD

Based on *Age of the Dinosaur* by Steve Parker, first published by the Natural History Museum, London, 2011

ISBN 978 0 565 09579 6

Designed by Bobby Birchall, Bobby&Co.
Reproduction by Saxon Digital Services
Printed by Toppan Leefung Printing Limited, China
Front cover: *Gigantosaurus* © Trustees of the Natural History Museum, London
Back cover: *Tarbosaurus* ©Friedrich Saurer/ Science Photo Library

This book is printed using 100% mineral free oil inks

MIX
Paper | Supporting responsible forestry
FSC® C104723
FSC www.fsc.org